Norfolk Orig

C000178651

2: ROADS & TRACKS

By Bruce Robinson and Edwin J. Rose
in collaboration with the Norfolk Museums Service

Map: Susan White
Illustrations: Susan White and Denise Derbyshire
Aerial Photograph: Derek A. Edwards

Poppyland Publishing

Other title in Norfolk Origins series:
1: Hunters to First Farmers (published 1981).

Text and drawings   Poppyland Publishing, Cromer, 1983
ISBN: 0 946148 04 X
Published by Poppyland Publishing, Cromer, 1983
Designed and produced by Speedprint Design, Spalding, Lincolnshire
Printed in Great Britain

Warning
Reference to or representation of a site, track or road should not be taken
as evidence that such a site, track or road can be seen or may be visited.
In many cases sites are on private land. Not all Roman roads are rights of
way

Dating
The following standard is employed:
BC   represents approximate calendrical date
b.c.   represents radio-carbon date

Contents

Castle Acre from the air. The Roman road (Peddars Way) enters the village (bottom) after crossing the River Nar. It re-emerges (top) to continue its journey across West Norfolk. (Derek A. Edwards, Norfolk Archaeological Unit, 1974).

Introduction

Most tracks, lanes and roads are undated and indeed virtually undatable, one reason being that very few retain their original purpose. Even fewer retain their original appearance. Instead, these corridors of movement might be better described as layer upon layer of modification, change of use, abandonment and re-use; as 'sandwiches' of complex uncertainty wherein dates and origins have become obscure and often quite meaningless.

The problem may be expressed another way. For example, is a Neolithic track still a Neolithic track if, after hundreds of years and hundreds of alterations, the route is now a trunk road? If so, then the busy A11 from Norwich to Thetford is not the A11 at all but a 17th and 18th century turnpike; or perhaps an Iron Age path.

Tracks and roads change, substantially and continually. They arise from an initial need, journey across countryside and pass landmarks which do not necessarily offer clues as to what that initial need or purpose was; and once in being, exert influence and sometimes a character all of their own.

It is a very thick sandwich indeed, and an understanding of the complexity may require a subtle change in attitude and an approach somewhat different from the traditional way in which we look at tracks and roads. This is especially so in relation to the pre-Roman period.

The Icknield Way is a prime example. The single track concept - often supported and/or justified by mapping the locations of find spots - is becoming much less viable. For one thing, it is now realised that a study of the distribution of find spots is not necessarily the most accurate foundation on which to base such opinions. For example, distribution maps give no clue as to what is still waiting to be found.

Aside from the tracks and trails of pre-history (and with the exception of engineered Roman roads, no roads or tracks in use before the 19th century had proper surfaces) the general history of road construction might usefully be divided into three phases: Roman, Turnpike and modern Motorway, or in the case of Norfolk which does not possess a single foot of motorway, modern Bypass.

It is these comparatively short periods of activity, and the considerably longer periods of inactivity between them, that we hope to examine in the light of current knowledge and understanding.

What this booklet offers is a sample of the available archaeological evidence. It will be understood at once, therefore, that seekers after ley-lines will find little support or comfort here. While it does seem probable that some stones or landmarks were used for guidance or as boundary marks there is no evidence that such a system was in widespread use as a general means of navigation.

Indeed, we hope it will become clear that humans (and animals for that matter) have been and still are too adaptable, too ingenious and too restless to remain trapped within or satisifed by the rigid limitations of straight lines.

Pre-Roman Tracks

About 8000 b.c. the cold climate of the Late Glacial finally and slowly evolved into the milder though still cold conditions of the Middle Stone Age, or the Mesolithic period. As the ice retreated so the meltwaters deposited boulders, gravel and silt over a landscape ravaged, crushed and scoured by the sheets and now pulled apart by the dramatic effects of a freeze/thaw climate. Slowly, too, woodlands of birch and pine replaced the copses of the tundra. Eastern England was still joined to the Continent by the 'Northsealand' land bridge. Many hundreds of years were to pass before Britain was finally an island.

Because of the known sequence of periods of glaciation - which included the Anglian, the Wolstonian and finally the Devensian - and because of the known and calculated effects of ice and climate on the landscape, it is reasonable to assume that the very oldest tracks in this area can be no more than 10,000 years old. Before that date the ice would have wiped the landscape clean of the marks of man.

Even so, none of the oldest known tracks have been positively dated to the Mesolithic period.

The people of the Early and Late Mesolithic periods were hunter-gatherers who in our area evidently lived in small communities similar to those perceived at sites such as Kelling Heath (on a high, sandy heathland), Plantation Farm and Peacock's Farm (Shippea Hill), in the fen margins, and on Wensum valley sites at Hellesdon, Sparham and Lyng. Some of them may have hunted auroch (wild ox) and deer and caught fish. What is certain is that the hunter groups were of necessity highly mobile, covering great distances as they followed the game, kept watch on the animal trails and watering places, and moved from one seasonal site to another.

Although the precise relationship between man, the environment and the seasonal movements of the game is still not wholly understood, it is appreciated that during the Mesolithic period, as through most pre-Roman periods, man knew the landscape well and understood it.

At the same time it is possible that the Mesolithic population was too small to have created and sustained tracks. Instead, the hunters may simply have wandered at will over the landscape, rather as Bushmen do today. If this is so then the only real tracks of this period were those created 'naturally' by animals.

When settled villages first began to appear in the Neolithic period (which opened about 3500 b.c.) there undoubtedly developed a need for regular lines of communication, for although hunting practices survived for a long time the gradual development of farming techniques and the attainment of a farming lifestyle began to forge stronger links between people and places. Thus the first permanent tracks began to appear.

Indeed, what started as a shifting form of agriculture evolved, as forest clearance increased, into a system of developing permanence. There would have been an increasing degree of purposeful direction, a greater need for systems of tracks to serve settlements, ritual sites, fields, rivers, coastal areas and animals; and a greater need for longer paths for trade.

That goods - including the products of local flint industries - were traded over long distances is certain. It is less certain that they were carried along main trading routes radiating, as some have suggested, from Wiltshire. It is even possible that river and coastal shipping was as important if not more important than the land haulage business. In any event the people of the Neolithic period were widespread and the population was expanding, many of them concentrating, as far as this area was concerned, along the eastern edge of the fens bordering the surmised 'line' of the Icknield Way (3) *

The Way was undoubtedly in use during the Neolithic period, but there is little evidence to suggest that it existed - in Norfolk, anyway - as a single and continuous track. Indeed, it is unlikely to have done so. Obstructions, diversions, alternating weather conditions and the need to cross watercourses and different terrains would almost certainly have brought alternative tracks into being at a very early stage.

There is some evidence, for example, that between Gayton Thorpe and Grimston the Way had at least one 'all weather' track slightly to the east of a marginally shorter 'summer' track which is basically followed by the line of the present B1153 road. Both these 'tracks' are close to the spring line, an important resource later utilised by the Romans. On the other hand an enigmatic enclosure recently excavated at Gallows Hill, near Thetford, and right on the theoretical line of the Icknield Way, produced no evidence of any major trackway.

It is difficult to conclude how important the Icknield Way was, or indeed, if it was important at all. It might have been a trading artery. Again, there could have been other more important lines of

(* Figures in parenthesis relate to the map at the end of the book. The Icknield Way and the Great Fen Road, both subsequently Romanised, are also included in the Roman text section).

communication, now completely lost and forgotten.

Whatever the truth of the matter it is clear that by c 2000 b.c., towards the end of the Neolithic period, East Anglia was established as a region of stock breeders and farmers.

Many of the Neolithic tracks would have remained useful throughout the Bronze Age, a period which saw settlements sometimes develop as small groups of thatched round houses surrounded by palisades set among well ordered and perhaps hedge-lined fields. By now field and track were thoroughly integrated. So, no doubt, were the arteries of trade which saw not only the passing of itinerant smiths but later, and during the Iron Age, the passage of wheeled transport and animals and the haulage of ore, tools, weapons, luxury goods and salt.

An expanding population and an increasing degree of trade and social order would also have brought an increasing sophistication in matters of travel and communication. The landscape was opening out. Iron Age constructions at places like Warham, South Creake, Holkham and Narborough testify to a degree of social organisation. Thus many of the tracks and paths of this period were the products not of the wanderings of hunters but of growth and development.

At the same time, obstacles and wear and tear from weather, hoof and wheel, must have caused the unrepaired tracks to continually disintegrate and thus 'wander'. Another blow to the ley-line theory, perhaps.

As we said earlier, surprisingly few of these pre-Roman tracks can or have been dated by archaeological evidence. Thus many claims are dubious. Nevertheless, it is clear that the peoples of the post-Devensian glaciation period were technically advanced and commercially developed. The tracks and trails which criss-crossed the land must have mirrored these activities.

The Icknield Way (3)

The Icknield Way could have had its origins in animal migration routes perhaps about 8000 b.c. In any event the upper and lower reaches of the chalk ridge seem to have provided a means of communication and to have been an area of some significance over a period of many hundreds of years. In terms of the Icknield's pre-Roman appearance, however, it needs to be seen not as a single path striding along the chalk ridge but as a corridor of numerous straggling tracks wandering roughly in the same direction.

Over the years it has provided a great many problems of interpretation, one of the largest being the actual direction taken, particularly between Newmarket and Thetford, and north of Thetford. For example, some Victorian writers suggested that it ran from

Thetford to Norwich, largely basing their claims on a track called Green Lane which diverges from the Way at Thetford. Although not the main route, Green Lane could possibly be contemporary with the Way.

Reconstruction of a pre-Roman trackway. This is how parts of the Icknield Way might have looked.

In 1923, and during a period of considerable antiquarian debate, W. G. Clarke put forward the suggestion of a chalk ridge route taking the Way from Thetford over what is now the Stanford Battle Area and across north-west Norfolk towards Hunstanton. Thus the concept of a single track (perhaps running all the way from Wiltshire to the coast) was also lent considerable substance.

The matter is still not wholly resolved. It is not known for certain, for example, if the Way did actually reach the coast. It may have petered out on Ringstead Downs. Again, another recent suggestion is that the Ordnance Survey-marked Way in the north-west of the county may in fact be Medieval, in which case the older pre-Roman tracks may have been further to the west and closer to the sea.

Some of the Icknield tracks were utilised by the Romans who settled and farmed this portion of the county to a quite considerable extent.

The origin of the name Icknield is not known, but it has been suggested it is derived from Iceni: i.e., the road leading to their land. As Norfolk people were referred to as 'Ikenny' as late as the 1950s this seems quite plausible. It may also be a generic name for Medieval tracks. The track in the Midlands known as Ryknield Street takes its name from the Icknield Way.

Tracks

Although Iron Age trackways probably contribute more lines to modern maps than any other human factor most of them are now quite undatable and unrecognisable. Over the centuries they have been subject to constant modification, re-use and obliteration.

There are many pieces of track and road (such as Green Bank near Ringstead) which may pre-date the Roman period. Another possibility is a 100-yard fragment of undated trackway between Larlingford and the former airfield at Snetterton (30). A somewhat larger example is Norwich Long Lane, Fakenham (31), now a modern lane and earmarked for alteration as part of Fakenham's proposed bypass. Passing to the north of the town Norwich Long Lane runs from close to Waterden (later to be on the line of a Roman road) by West Barsham and Lodge Farm, only to peter out near the Saxon cemetery at Pensthorpe Hall.

One more example is the Great Fen Road (2), or East Harling Drove. The fen edges have proved exceedingly rich in pre-Roman material, and the Great Fen Road seems to have had its beginnings at Blackdyke, near Hockwold, which was once a dyke leading to the sea. From Hockwold its line can be traced by Weeting, north of Santon Downham, and roughly as far as the railway line near Bridgham not far from where it crosses the Roman Peddars Way. It may have progressed further towards East Harling. It would also, of course, have crossed the line of the Icknield Way and gone to within a short distance of the Grimes Graves flint mines complex.

It is possible that the Great Fen Road dates from the Neolithic period. Later, it was in part altered and improved by the Romans; later still, it became a drovers' road.

Fords

A widespread pre-Roman use of fords is inferred and presumed. The continuing use and importance of crossing places is also suggested by post-Roman names such a Larlingford, Wayford, Thetford, Stanford, Lackford, Billingford, Narford and Sedgeford. Most fords were merely broad and shallow places where the trails of men and animals converged.

As with tracks, there is great difficulty in actually proving the use of a ford in a particular period. Very few fords have been dated with accuracy. A number of pre-Roman fords are known to have existed on the Thames, for example, but as far as Norfolk is concerned

The Great Fen Road, or East Harling Drove. Pre-Roman, later Romanised, later still a drovers' road.

archaeological evidence of actual prehistoric use is very slight.

One possible example is a ford at Narford (it would have been on or near one of the suggested lines of the Icknield Way, and also close to Iron Age earthworks) which shows some evidence of metalling. This may be Iron Age or it may merely indicate a Roman re-use of the same crossing place.

Perhaps the best Norfolk example is the site now occupied by the town of Thetford which sits astride the rivers Little Ouse and Thet and which, for hundreds of years, has been an important crossing place. Earthworks at Castle Hill also help to indicate a pre-Roman importance. Possible crossing places have been suggested in five areas of Thetford - Red Castle, Nun's Bridges, Thetford Bridge, and one mile east and one mile west of the town. None, however, has been dated.

Incidentally, the name Thetford is thought to mean 'peoples' ford' or 'the ford everybody uses'.

Stones

The suggested use of mark-stones or puddingstones (conglomerates) as sight-lines is not proved and must be treated with suspicion. In any event pre-historic tracks, human or animal, did not maintain a straight line for very long. Rather, they tended to be rambling and improvised.

There are many glacial erratics in Norfolk, no doubt left behind by the meltwaters of departing ice. Some may have been moved from their original position, while a good number (eg, the Stockton Stone, the Great Stone of Lyng, and Harold's Stone at Harleston) have local legends and significance. (See also, Cowell Stone; Roman: milestones). None, however, has a proved connection with a road.

Roman Roads

In AD 43, almost a century after the initial reconnaissance, the Romans under Claudius rapidly conquered the south eastern portion of the British Isles.

They found a landscape different from that of today, though largely tamed and extensively settled and cultivated. The Wash, for example, ran deeper into the land than it does at present. Most of the fenland area was already there, but again, the area of marshland did not extend quite as far north as it does today. Except in Breckland, a substantial amount of forest probably survived, too. East and west of Norwich, for example, there were thick woods until at least the late Middle Ages.

The Romans also found a landscape marked and criss-crossed by innumerable tracks. Indeed, much of the Roman army's early exploration and its initial military thrusts must have been carried out along existing Iron Age tracks.

The Icknield Way was already of great age (its origins in time being further from the Romans than the Roman period is from us) and doubtless, and in the opinion of the conquerors, in dire need of improvement and repair. In the event a requirement for proper roads with metalled surfaces was quickly established. The decision to plan such a network, no doubt developed with the needs of the military foremost in mind, set in motion what may be described as the first great age of road building.

Documentary evidence

One record, in the form of a diagrammatic sketch map, is provided by the Tabula Peutingeriana (the Peutinger Table) the original of which is believed to date from the 3rd century. On the 13th century copy, which is all that survives, the Roman Empire is drawn on a series of sheets fastened as a long roll. Alas, most of Britain was on the outermost sheet, which is lost, though a small portion of the south and east coastal areas survives. As a map, however, it would appear to be somewhat inaccurate.

A more valuable source of information is the Itinerary of Antoninus (the Antonine Itineraries) of which Nos. V and IX pass through this region. Iter IX deals with a route from Venta Icenorum (Caistor St. Edmund) to Londinium (London) passing near or through Yoxford, Baylham House, Colchester, Chelmsford and Romford. The listed distance was a total of 127 Roman miles. A Roman mile was a thousand paces, or about one thousand yards (mille passum, hence 'mile').

Part of Iter V relates a circuitous route from London to Cambridge (Duroliponte) taking in Chelmsford, Colchester, Scole (Villa Faustini), Caistor St. Edmund (here called Icinos, which seems to have been an alternative name for Venta Icenorum) and Icklingham.

Incidentally, if the Romans did actually give names to the roads then none of the names has survived or has been recognised. Some of the names by which we know the roads today date from the Late Medieval period, while others may be even more recent inventions.

Dating

The dating of the construction of each road, and in consequence the actual sequence of construction, is not known. Nevertheless, the core period of activity would seem to have been centered around the second half of the 1st century. Indeed, R. R. Clarke ('East Anglia', EP

Publishing) dated the Scole-Caistor St. Edmund road to about AD 70. A coin of Vesparsian (Emperor, AD 69-79) was found in the metalling of the Fen Causeway, but this is likely to be due to later repairs. So although there is little doubt that modifications and additions to the network were continued throughout the period of the occupation, it seems reasonable to assume that the bulk of the construction work took place between AD 47 and c AD 100.

I. D. Margery ('Roman Roads in Britain', Baker) suggested a slightly earlier start, arguing that in the period of the initial conquest "we may consider the road-building effort as starting in the south east and south of Britain in AD 43".

What is clear is that road construction began very soon after the main invasion. It is probable, therefore, that among the first roads were those leading from the East Kent ports to London. The London-Chelmsford-Colchester road may also have been a fairly early construction, indicating that what subsequently became known as the Pye Road (Baylham House, Scole, Caistor St. Edmund) followed later as a logical extension. Once Braughing and Great Chesterford had been added to the system then the Icknield Way became readily available to the Romans, providing access to the eastern fringes of the fens and the eastern shores of the Wash. The Peddars Way, which runs almost parallel with the Icknield Way for much of its journey across Norfolk, may thus have been one of the earliest, if not the earliest, Roman road in the county.

Once the military impetus slowed other roads and tracks (eg, to link settlements, administration and trade centres, anchorages and farms) gradually began to appear. For example, the main east-west road (the Fen Causeway: Denver to Smallburgh) seems to date from the 2nd or 3rd century. However, until the final withdrawal of Roman forces (c AD 425) changing needs and circumstances ensured regular modification and expansion of the system.

The workers

The construction of roads, initially anyway, was a military responsibility. One reason for this may have been that a planned network of metalled surfaces, allowing for the easy passage of men, animals and materials in all weathers and at the greatest possible speed, was seen as an essential element of a military campaign. As a result the early surveys of the countryside may have been undertaken by surveyors who if they were not actually members of the army were at least attached to army units.

One suggestion is that some of the roads were built as part of a 'rolling' programme, the highways being part and parcel of military advances, actually being built as the troops moved forward. Some of the early main roads, such as the Peddars Way, certainly possess an air of having been built under military supervision, for construction methods and the presumed initial purpose of the road both suggest a high degree of military specification.

Reconstruction of Roman road-building methods. Note the 'sighting' system, and the cleared land on either side.

There is no evidence of any use of forced labour. Although Norfolk was a depressed area in AD 61 and for a short time after, relations between the native population and the Romans, though regularly strained, nevertheless seem to have been sustained at manageable levels before the revolt and restored quickly afterwards. Nevertheless, it is logical that a native work force was employed in some capacity. It is even possible that paid employment on the construction of the roads assisted recovery of the shattered post-revolution economy.

Aside from the military roads it is clear that some others were less weightily built or were built to 'non-military' specifications. This apparent lack of standardisation in design, materials and method could mean that particular groups, while still under overall supervision, were responsible for particular sections of roads or particular areas. Another possiblity is that some of the work was turned over to local 'contractors'. Either that, or military specifications were not applied, perhaps because major engineering was not required or was not appropriate. Another possibility is that the designs were amended or modified because of a need for financial economy.

Whatever the correct interpretation the construction of the county's network of main roads, minor roads, lanes and tracks, a task which must have been spread over many decades, required specialist knowledge, considerable organisation, capital investment, vast amounts of materials and a large and persistent work force.

Construction methods

It is not known if Roman surveyors and engineers possessed detailed maps, but they clearly gained an intimate knowlege of the landscape. In general their roads pay careful regard to obstacles, and although not always perfectly straight, display a preference for the shortest practical route. For example, the Peddars Way, in a distance of about 45 miles, makes only one major directional change, at Galley Hill, north-east of East Wretham. There was a Norfolk legend that the Way also turned at Ringstead and ended at St. Edmund's Point, Hunstanton, but this story may have been provoked by a side road diverging at this point towards Hunstanton.

The general 'straightness' is also assumed to be a result of careful sighting and surveying from one high point to another or from positions offering wide fields of vision. In some places existing pre-Roman tracks would have been pressed into service, improved and 'Romanised' (ie, the Icknield Way and the East Harling Drove, or Great Fen Road).

There seems to have been a number of different construction designs and a wide range of used materials. To a major degree the design was dictated by the terrain and by the road's actual purpose (eg, military, agricultural), while the basic rule for building material seems to have been formed, generally and logically, on what was available locally. Thus the Peddars Way was a substantial highway compared with the constructional poverty of some of the other roads and tracks in the county.

Interestingly, and despite the reliance on local material, there is rarely any indication of where these materials were obtained. Only a few pits have been found in the vicinity of roads, and none have been discovered in Norfolk.

In general, and once the line of a road had been decided and measured (the survey having taken place over a landscape littered with tracks and settlements) a wide belt of land was evidently cleared and prepared. Parallel outer ditches, or markers, perhaps as much as 90 ft apart, were sometimes ploughed or dug. In any event a centre line was marked, perhaps by a single furrow, and the inner core of the road built with materials sometimes scooped from a second line of parallel inner 'ditches' close to the road.

Once the inner core and scoop ditches were completed stones were often used to build up the agger (the actual embankment which carried the road) which was then cambered to assist drainage and 'metalled' with small stones or gravel.

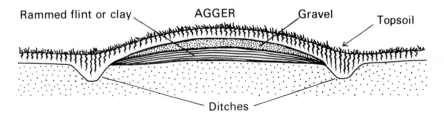

A cross-section of a Roman Road, showing the way some of them were built with local materials and then 'metalled' with small stones and gravel. The section also shows the modern outline of subsequent soil deposits and vegetation growth.

Some aggers were anywhere between 8 ft. and 50 ft. across, the larger ones presumably for double lines of traffic. There is a visible example of a short section of agger (private, fenced and somewhat overgrown) south of the river Thet at Brettenham, where it forms the western boundary of the Thorpe Woodlands (Foresty Commission) caravan and camping site. Perhaps the largest and best Norfolk example, again on the Peddars Way, is also on private land north of the wood north of the Brettenham-Bridgham road. There are a few more Peddars Way examples north of Shepherd's Bush.

Incidentally, this type of embankment gave rise to the term 'high road'.

Many of the local roads or lanes were little more than tracks. Others were more substantial constructions. One section of the Denver road (the Fen Causeway) was built on a foundation of oak trunks and branches, wattle, stones, and 2 ft. to 3 ft. of gravel aggregate. On the other hand when the line of the Peddars Way was cut by excavation equipment prior to the building of the Swaffham bypass, no sign of Roman work was discovered. It had either been destroyed by many years of agricultural activity, or this section of the road was originally built without an agger.

Elsewhere, this particular road has left more tangible traces. An archaeological excavation at Brettenham in the 1930's showed that here the road was 16 ft. wide, 2 ft. 6 in. thick in the centre, and built of

17

rammed flint topped with gravel. On the east side of the road a gravel pavement, or layby, continued for a further 4 ft. North of the river the agger was built largely of rammed chalky flint and boulder clay.

Bridges

Bridges, being expensive and time-consuming to build, and presumably vulnerable to attack, seem to have been provided only where no alternative was available. Comparatively few have been positively identified in this country. One example is on Ermine Street (Lincoln to London) where the road crossed the Nene west of Peterborough. This bridge may have been built of stone and timber. In another example at Alfoldean, West Sussex, oak piles were used.

The only bridge for which evidence has been found in Norfolk was situated at Downham West. It was excavated in 1933, and wooden post holes indicated that a bridge had indeed carried the Fen Causeway across what was once a stream and is now a roddon, or rodham - a silt bank, an extinct watercourse, left high and dry by the lowering of the surrounding land.

Fords

The crossing of water was a major problem and a major accomplishment. For example, between the Little Ouse river and the present village of Thompson, a distance of about ten miles, the Peddars Way crosses three rivers and several streams and marshy areas. Indeed, this particular road still crosses at least ten stretches of water in a total distance of about 45 miles.

In general fords were preferred to bridges, and several types seem to have been provided including a few which were paved, making a sort of underwater causeway, and a few with steps leading to the water. At least two on the Peddars Way - Blackwater Ford at Rushford and Droveway Ford at Brettenham - have retained their working titles for several hundred years.

It is sometimes the case that Roman roads on either side of a river or stream are not in precise alignment with the ford. Droveway Ford is one example. At Blackwater Ford the Roman engineers built a Z-bend, a fairly common device, to enable the road to approach the ford. Also, over the centuries and because of changing conditions, the most favourable crossing places would not necessarily remain in precisely the same place.

Incidentally, there is a 19th century account of a 'paved ford' across the river at Scole, but the location is not known. There are also various stories of roads paved with 'stone slabs'. If accurate, the stones must have been imported.

Milestones

A few Roman milestones have been found, though none have been definitely identified in Norfolk. Elsewhere, some have been in the shape of pillars and some cut as mounting blocks. A small number carried inscriptions.

Blomefield, in the 18th century, wrote of a large milestone 'lately to be seen on the Bury Road' at Ickburgh, though Haverfield (1901) was sceptical. The name 'Rome Stone' appears near Grimston, on a map of 1588, but the details are not known. Again, Tom Martin, the Thetford antiquary, wrote c 1740, 'An ancient stone at ye runne of water between Threxton and Saham Toney Query what it is?' As this might have been in the middle of the Woodcock Hall (Romano-British) settlement on the Peddars Way it is clearly a possibility.

The Cowell Stone, near Swaffham, which could have been set up in Roman times.

The Cowell Stone, to be found among the verge grasses on a narrow track a few yards north of the present Swaffham to Marham road, may also have been set up in Roman times. It could be a post-Roman boundary mark, but it does indicate the place where the east-to-west road (which continues the line of the Fen Causeway) crosses the Romanised Icknield Way. It also marks parish and Hundred boundaries. The stone itself is a glacial boulder and as such is not particularly rare.

As for the origin of the name it could be derived from the Saxon word 'doule', meaning boundary mark. On the other hand W. G. Clarke (1923) wrote that the name Cowell, or Growell, was recorded as present in nearby Beachamwell in the 13th century.

ROADS & TRACKS

Mileage

Because of lost and doubtful stretches a precise count of the total length of highways constructed by the Romans in this country is not possible. However, it is estimated that between 7000 and 10,000 miles of roads were built during a period which may have lasted less than 300 years.

In Norfolk the length of known Roman and Romanised roads and tracks amounts to about 240 miles, while a further 80 miles, at least, seem possible. The actual original mileage of Roman highways in the county may have been much higher.

The Roads

(**Note:** The figures in parenthesis refer to the map at the end of the book; the list does not include short sections excavated on sites, some of which may have been paths leading to places of work or residence).

Coney Weston to Attleborough (1). A continuation of the road from Ixworth, considered by Margery to have been built before the Peddars Way. Its route from East Harling is doubtful, but it may have gone along Haverscroft Street to Attleborough. Indeed, there is a good example of agger to the north-east of the town. Its original termination is not known.

Hockwold to Roudham (2). Already mentioned in the pre-Roman section. Known as the Great Fen Road or the East Harling Drove. It is a Romanised trackway which passed through a district in Santon Warren which was probably heavily occupied at the time. It crossed the Icknield Way and the Peddars Way.

Icknield Way (3). Again, a trackway straightened and Romanised. Margery concluded it entered the area at Lackford, formed the south-east boundary of Elvedon Park and continued beyond Thetford to Croxton Park. From there the line went from Mouse Hall to Stanford, Smugglers' Road, Hilborough, Cockley Cley, Narford Hall, East Walton, Gayton Thorpe, Shernbourne and Ringstead Downs. There is no evidence of any course north of Ringstead Downs.

Scole to Caistor St. Edmund, the Pye Road (4). Evidently known as the Pye Road since the 18th century, the name may derive from an inn called the Magpie at Little Stonham. The course more or less follows the present main road to Dunston, except at Dickleburgh. Here the modern road diverges round the Moor while the Roman road went straight on. In the last century a claim was made that the Roman road crossed a 'crannog', an artificial lake dwelling. Its route near Newton Flotman is also uncertain, but there was a ford near the bridge. Passing through the grounds of Dunston Hall the road reached the river opposite the west gate of Venta, to which it may have been connected by a bridge.

Peasenhall (to Pulham St. Mary?) (5). The route was close to Ubbeston and Fressingfield and south-east of Weybread to the river Waveney. There was a Roman settlement at Needham, so the road may have crossed the river into Norfolk, possibly as far as Pulham St. Mary.

Halesworth to Woodton, known as Stone Street (6). This road may have connected with Yoxford or Dunwich at one end and Venta at the other. Its course is followed by a modern road as far as Woodton, but it then diverged to the west side of Brooke Wood.

Arminghall to Kirby Bedon (7). Known as Blind Lane in the 16th century, it may have run north-east from Arminghall, south of Bixley Hall and through the grounds of Kirby Bedon Hall. It is possible it originated at Venta and could have served as a connection between Venta and the river.

Smallburgh to Denver (8). This route is the eastern end of the Fen Causeway that begins near Peterborough, and is apparently continued by a road as far as Smallburgh and perhaps to Caister-on-Sea. It has not been traced with certainty east of Smallburgh. Excavations at Wayford Bridge in the 1970s revealed a road built of soil topped with cobbles, and through the soil bank a box construction of wooden beams lined by tree stumps. A boat-like structure was radio-carbon dated to c AD 210. There are three undated fords at Wayford. West of Smallburgh the course of the road ran through Sloley to Fairstead, through the grounds of Scottow Hall and then to the river Bure. From Brampton it continued to Marsham Heath, crossed the present Norwich to Holt road, and on to Jordan Green, Bawdeswell and Billingford. Stony Lane and Salters Lane carried it by Bittering towards Kempstone and then to Bartholomews Hills near where, south of Castle Acre, it crossed the Peddars Way. The Fincham Drove led it towards Swaffham Heath, over the Icknield Way (by the Cowell Stone) and on to Downham Market and Denver. At Denver Sluice, where there was a large salt-working settlement, the east-west road became the Fen Causeway running via Nordelph, Upwell Fen and South District towards March. In this area there may have been several parallel courses of differing dates, but they are hard to tell from roddons. It is worth noting that at Brampton the crossroads was staggered, excavation showing that the road did not go straight on. One explanation may be that the east-west road was constructed in sections at different times.

Holkham to Toftrees (9). It ran south from the coast, forming the west boundary of Holkham Park and the Hundred boundary.

Toftrees to North Elmham (10). This road ran through Toftrees via Horningtoft, where it was re-used as a manor park boundary, to North

Elmham. Several other short lengths of road radiate from Toftrees, which is an important Roman site.

Toftrees to Pickenham (11). The course of the road from Toftrees was through East Raynham to Pickenham, where it joined the Peddars Way. It was still visible as a mound in the last century when it was known as Walsingham Way. A good piece of agger remains in woods at Lexham Park.

Brisley to King's Lynn (12). A possible Roman road which would have formed a branch of the main east-west road. It has been suggested it may have continued as far as Cowbit, near Spalding.

Norwich, east to west (13). The line of this road has been traced from Bawburgh through Bowthorpe, along what is now Dereham Road and St. Andrew's Street, under the cathedral, along Bishopgate, Gas Hill, St. William's Way and on to Thorpe.

Dickleburgh to Tivetshall (14). This road diverged from the Pye Road at Dickleburgh and ran on to a Roman villa at Tivetshall. The modern road follows it from Dickleburgh centre to the first bend where it diverges from the Pye Road to avoid the Moor.

Billingford to Sparham Hole (15). Yet another road diverging from the east-west road. It followed a course from Billingford, along Bylaugh Park and on to Sparham Hole and the river.

Fragments of other known Roman roads include:

(16) a possible branch from the Peddars Way at Ringstead towards Old Hunstanton;

(17) a possible link between the Peddars Way and Brancaster;

(18) east-west roads from Little Barwick to Egmere, and from Crabbe's Castle through Wighton towards Binham;

(19) a north-south link from Brampton to Thorpe St. Andrew (a Roman settlement site), it followed the route of the modern roads, including Thunder Lane;

(20) a fragment of an east-west road at Scole;

(21) a section which connected Gooderstone, South Pickenham and Ashill, it passed through a gap in the Panworth Ditch earthwork and ran alongside Robin Hood's Garden Roman enclosure, while just west of the latter another road ran SW-NE for a short distance;

(22) an east-west road through Watton on the line of the modern road, with a possible branch at the west end towards Clermont House and beyond;

(23) Mattishall (Stone Road) running to the NW of the village for about half a mile;

(24) a road running NW from Caistor St. Edmund, it forms the modern road through Keswick and in the last century was visible as an earthwork continuing to Caistor;

(25) various short stretches running east, SE and NE from Caistor

St. Edmund;

(26) a north-south stretch forming a parish boundary under the aerials at Upper Stoke, and in 1590 referred to as Stone Street;

(27) a possible north-south road for a short distance on the west side of Stanfield;

(28) and a short north-south section east of Hempnall at Street Wood.

(**Note:** A crop-mark of a possible Roman road has been recorded running from near Wicklewood towards Caistor St. Edmund. At the time of writing, however, this has not been accurately plotted).

Peddars Way (29). The Peddars Way, which forks from the Ixworth road near Stanton Chare and runs for over 45 miles to the north-west Norfolk coast, is the most important, most substantial and best surviving example of a Roman road in Norfolk.

It is considered to be of military proportions, and its original purpose may have been to assist the expedition of troops and supplies across the Wash and to allow easier access to the eastern edges of the fens and the chalk ridge of west Norfolk. Its seaward termination is thought to have been at or near Holme-next-Sea, though its actual approach to the coast was slightly to the west of where the Ordnance Survey and the modern street name marks it.

It rises slowly and gently from below 100 ft. (Little Ouse and Thet rivers) to about 350 ft. (Shepherd's Bush, near Castle Acre) before falling again to sea level. The general line of its progress is slightly to the east of and usually higher than the Icknield Way, though towards the northern extremity the routes move to within two miles of each other.

Some sections of the Way have been lost so that it is no longer a continuous path. However, it still offers a variety of surfaces ranging from modern metalled roads, stony farm tracks, grassy lanes and forest paths of flint and light soil. In some sections it has almost become a hollow way, particularly in the north, while in other places the agger is still visible. Another short section north of Harpley Dams - where the land is basically high and dry - currently gives the impression of having been built on an embankment, with a drop on the east side of several feet.

About 50 per cent of the Peddars Way still marks various parish boundaries.

Suggestions that north of Castle Acre the road coincided with a pre-Roman track cannot be ruled out, but there is no archaeological evidence to support the theory. The Peddars Way is crossed by several other Roman roads and it is presumed there were connecting roads, lanes and tracks probably branching off in both directions but certainly to the west towards the Icknield Way.

The road's basic directness and feeling of urgency is a continual reminder of its military background, and the present gentle curve at Galley Hill (about 150 ft. about sea level) represents the only major change in direction made along its entire length. Faden's map of Norfolk (1797) suggests this junction of tracks and paths has changed considerably over the years, while Margery has pointed out that slight mounds in the bends of the road (visible in the Forestry Commission plantations) may be traces of agger. The matter is uncertain. For example, Galley Hill is a parish boundary, and similar slight mounds at the side of the Way can be found along the verges and hedgerows of a stretch not far from Bircham, which is also a parish boundary. Furrows and mounds are not unusual on forestry land.

Whether or not the original purpose of the Peddars Way did rapidly evaporate is not known, but it is clear that settlements of various sizes developed near the road at places like Stanton Chare (Suffolk), Brettenham, Threxton/Woodcock Hall and Sedgeford/Fring. It is tempting to suggest they might have developed from regularly spaced posting stations where travellers and horses found rest and nourishment, but the positions of some of them (eg, Brettenham, Threxton/Woodcock Hall) seems determined by the positions of rivers rather than by any regulation distance. At the same time it is puzzling why Castle Acre, situated on high ground and thus commanding an important crossroads and river crossing, has produced only slight evidence of Roman activity. On the other hand there is some evidence for a very early military fort at Woodcock Hall.

The name Peddars Way is probably a Late Medieval attachment and seems to be little more than a generic name for a footpath, rather as 'roadway' is an all-embracing label. It has been applied to many other paths. For example, a stretch of the Icknield Way in the area of Hilborough was evidently referred to as 'Pedderysty alias Saltersty' during the reign of Henry IV.

Sections of the Peddars Way are included in proposals for a Countryside Commission long distance footpath, which, if implemented, would run from Knettishall to Hunstanton and along the coast to Cromer.

Conclusions

Without precise knowledge of dating and sequence it is difficult to reach conclusions as to the original purpose of the roads although it is reasonable to assume that some, built in the years just before or just after the Boudican revolt, were laid down first for military and then for administrative reasons. Thus it could be argued that the Peddars Way, quite plainly a military road of importance, may have been the first Roman road in the area.

24

Although there are obvious similarities with the Icknield Way (the line of the Icknield was later developed by the Romans) the Peddars Way is unlikely to have been a simple replacement. These two lines of communication spring from quite different sources and seem to have served totally different purposes. Whereas the line of the Icknield Way kept largely to the lower western slopes of the chalk ridge and meandered from farm to farm and settlement to settlement, the Peddars Way hugged the generally higher route and was apparently made for fast transport, not for farm carts.

Tracks and paths almost certainly linked the two, but the Peddars Way seems to have been built to assist the policing of the area and to facilitate the transit of troops and supplies. If ferry or anchorage facilities were available in the Wash then troops from Lincoln or Colchester, for example, could have been moved quicky north or south, avoiding the fens in the process; conversely, they could have been rushed to the area in the event of disturbances in the fens or the Midlands.

Aside from the Peddars Way it is possible that a regular military requirement for Norfolk's road faded at a comparatively early date. It is easy, for example, to visualise the Pye Road busy with expense-account administrators commuting between Colchester and Caistor St. Edmund. In the same way, and during the long years of comparative peace and prosperity, it is also possible to see the great east-west road (from Denver to Smallburgh, and presumably to Caister on Sea) handling the pottery produce of Brampton, farm produce from the west Norfolk farms, salt from Denver and cargoes from the coast.

In this context Brampton might be seen as an important crossroads: north to the Wash and the sea, south to Caistor St. Edmund, Colchester and London, west to Water Newton and the Midlands, east to Caister on Sea and the coast. Brampton, in fact, was a busy place with lots of little streets, a bank and a ditch, and industrial suburbs.

Other communities also grew beside the roads - a few of them no doubt springing from posting stations or even earlier pre-Roman settlements - and it is clear that the landscape became a busy patchwork of communities, farmsteads and fields.

The possibility of harbours or anchorages (and a ferry) off the Norfolk coast has already been mentioned. The direction of the Peddars Way suggests there may have been something of the sort near Holme. If this is so, the general coastward approach of the Toftrees to Holkham road, for example, could suggest a similar coastal purpose. If such facilities did exist then some of the landing places may have been in areas now covered by the sea. It is worth noting that north east Norfolk has so far produced comparatively few traces of

Roman roads, a largely blank portion of the map which in general coincides with poor areas for anchorages.

During the centuries of Roman occupation and pacification there slowly grew a fully integrated national network - many of the roads radiating from London - which linked towns, camps, minor centres and agricultural and industrial areas. Beside them there also grew and developed the many cross links and feeder roads and lanes which served local purposes and which no doubt complemented the existing network of tracks which were old even when the Romans came.

The Roman achievement must not be under-estimated. They laid down the very first pattern of 'metalled' roads, and when they finally departed some 1200 years were to pass before anyone tried anything of the sort again. Even today many of our motor roads follow routes laid down by the surveyors of Claudius.

Turnpikes and Bypasses

The Roman roads lay unrepaired and largely untouched for centuries, decaying slowly throughout the Saxon and Medieval periods. It is presumed the surfaces disintegrated first, followed at length by the bridges. Some of the smaller Roman tracks may have disappeared altogether or become overgrown. Stone robbing must also have contributed to a general deterioration.

As immigrants and farmers rather than invaders and conquerors the Saxons lacked the wealth and the authority of Rome. They tended to develop small self-contained communities rather than wide national interests. So the road pattern changed again. Having settled in an existing Romanised landscape the Saxons were largely content with unmade roads. Only those portions of the Roman network relevant to the Saxon way of life were brought into regular use.

In general, however, the roads decayed because many were not relevant (Saxons on mules did not need highways of Roman size and directness) and because there was no strong central government to say So-and-so must repair this piece or that piece; and provide the cash to pay them to do it. A modern parallel can be found in certain North African countries where broad straight roads built by the French now have gaps in them where the bridges have fallen.

Thus many of the Early Saxon villages seem to shun the Roman roads, being sited away from the main routes. In north west Norfolk, Fring, Bircham and Massingham all seem purposely to ignore the presence of the Peddars Way a few miles to the west. Later settlements were linked by tracks that may have begun as driftways for cattle. Indeed, some village 'back lanes' may have started life as driftways at a time when stock was driven to fields and commons. This was because farmhouses tended to be clustered together and not scattered, as today. Towards the end of the Saxon period, however, villages began to grow beside the roads once more.

It is clear that throughout the Middle Ages (and other than in walled towns, or particular short stretches) roads were not built purposely and directly from A to B. Instead, they came into being as and when they were needed, and abandoned when circumstances changed.

The period also saw the use of uncultivated strips to delineate fields. In time the tracks along these grass strips became more or less permanent. This is one reason why bends can sometimes be found in roads which tend to follow parish boundaries. Of course, the cost of maintaining the tracks was still a local responsibility, and it was because of the implied importance of maintaining boundaries that the ceremony of 'beating the bounds' became of such significance.

The granting of fairs and markets, the growth of the abbeys and monasteries, and the sporting interests of the nobles, gave impetus to travel in the 12th and 13th centuries.

The Statute of Winchester, 1252, laid down that highways connecting market towns should be widened so that there was no ditch, undergrowth or tree in which a mischief-maker might lurk within 200 ft. of either side (great oaks and beeches excluded). Roads under the King's protection were already supposed to be wide enough for the passing of two waggons.

The effect of bad weather is best left to the imagination. In some cases and because of bad weather, bad road conditions, or obstacles, parallel side roads and tracks came into use. So the wide roads, originally introduced for the safety of the public, were retained when wheeled transport became more common. Nevertheless, the winding Medieval lanes were clearly in a bad state and quite unsuitable for a world in which trade and travel were increasing.

Bridges

Some Roman bridges undoubtedly survived for a long time, but it is likely they had largely decayed by the time of the Conquest. However, with the increase in influence of the church, and the pull of the markets, a new need arose. A slow transition from ford to wooden bridge, and from wooden bridge to stone bridge, was thus quite common.

Bridges also provoked many acrimonious disputes, quite often over the question of maintenance. It was held that the Common Law of England required that whoever built a bridge was also responsible for its good repair. The arguments were often further bedevilled by boundary disputes. Sometimes the boundary ran down the centre of the stream in question.

A great many bridges were built, however, many of them by benevolent individuals, because one useful answer to the problem of cost and upkeep was to designate bridge construction and repair as 'pious and meritorious works before God'. One Norfolk example of this is St. Olave's Bridge, the original of which was built as a religious offering by the wife of Sir Henry Hobart, Chancellor to Henry VII. Sir Henry, in turn, built Loddon church.

Bishop Bridge, in Norwich, is an example of a Medieval bridge, but it is not typical because it was built as part of the city defences. One very unusual bridge is in the grounds of Walsingham Priory. It may be the only surviving packhorse bridge in Norfolk.

An unusual bridge in the grounds of Walsingham Priory, it may be a surviving packhorse bridge (Pic: Edwin J. Rose).

Pilgrim tracks

Very few roads and tracks are thought to have been developed for a single purpose (there are no known salt roads in Norfolk, for example) and the same point has to be made about pilgrim roads and tracks. One of the best known in the country is the Pilgrims' Way leading to Canterbury, a prehistoric route which acquired its present name because there was no other way for the pilgrims to go. The same is not the case as far as the Walsingham Way is concerned.

The amount of 'traffic' generated by the pilgrims of the Middle Ages was considerable, and in turn led to the need for lodgings and hospices. In this way, it is thought, inns developed.

As far as Walsingham is concerned, however, there is little evidence other than an oral tradition to support the single-track concept. It seems more likely that in Norfolk almost every village had its 'Walsingham Way' or 'Pilgrim Way' because almost every village had a road along which pilgrims, arriving from all parts of the compass, would pass on their journey to and from Walsingham.

A modern comparison of this would be to point out that almost every village in east Norfolk has a Yarmouth Road; but if the phrase 'Yarmouth Road' is used in isolation then it is usually understood to mean the A47. In much the same way some pilgrim routes - like Mount Ephraim, near Weeting - were busier and perhaps more important than others, and were marked with stones or crosses. However, although fragments of pilgrim roads and Pilgrim Ways do remain, they do not necessarily constitute a continuous path.

Other similar names (eg, Procession Way, east of Swaffham and a part of the Peddars Way) are more likely connected with the ceremony of beating the bounds.

Turnpikes

For a long time the condition of the country's roads and tracks was very poor indeed. About 1600 the Bury-to-Thetford road was basically a track across a sandy heath. One hundred and fifty years' later there had not been much improvement, for the way between Thetford and Brandon, for example, was still a sandy waste which brought great discomfort to travellers. As for the road at Bawsey Bottom, on the present B1145 between King's Lynn and Gayton, it was said to be the worst in all England in winter.

The problem revolved around a general lack of overall policy, firm surfaces and proper and regular repairs. Indeed, many landowners came to regard as a curse those long distance travellers who, because of the conditions, were forced to stray or detour from the roads in order to avoid difficult or impassable areas.

A Highway Act of 1555 set out to improve matters. It provided that two parishioners should be elected annually at a parish session to act as highway surveyors to inspect roads and bridges three times a year and to report deficiencies. It also ordered that every person holding land of an annual value of £50 or more was required to provide two men, a team of horses or oxen, tools and implements, to repair the highway for eight hours on four consecutive days each year. For obvious reasons the Act was unpopular. It was not entirely successful, either. It failed to specify standards or offer incentives.

Harrison's 'Description' (1577-86) showed the main local highways of this period as: London-Ware-Walsingham and London-Colchester-Yarmouth. This is an incomplete picture, however. In 1635 Jacob van Langeren's 'Direction for the English Traviller - Northfolke', included a distance/mileage chart for 26 Norfolk towns and villages.

Some 35 years later, with more roads beginning to appear on more maps, W. Hollar's map of Norfolk picked out: Brandon-Swaffham-Holkham, Thetford-Attleborough-Norwich, Diss-Norwich, King's Lynn-Brisley-Norwich, King's Lynn-Swaffham, Norwich-Aylsham-Cromer, Norwich-Worstead-Cromer, and Norwich-Loddon-Yarmouth.

One description of the Medieval route from London to Norwich suggested that travellers, on reaching Newmarket, were faced with three possibilities - the present A11 via Barton Mills; Kennett, Herringswell, Tuddenham (Suffolk) and Temple Bridge; or along the line of the present A45 to Cavenham and on to Icklingham or Lackford. Travelling across Breckland the routes converged at Thetford where three or more alternatives were offered - the present A11, a route via Bridgham, and a third option by East Wretham. They all converged at or near Attleborough before proceeding to Norwich.

Improvements had to be made, and in 1663 there was a further important Highway Act. It provided for the repair of highways within the counties of Hertford, Cambridge and Huntingdon (on the line of the Great North Road) and for the introduction of tolls. The country's first tollgate was installed at Wadesmill in Hertfordshire.

Thus the second great age of road building, the Turnpike Age, was born. It was the first serious attempt since the Romans to introduce a national programme of construction.

By about 1700 seven Turnpike Trusts had been created in various parts of the country, but the rate of creation quickened throughout the 18th century until during the final decade Acts were going through Parliament at the rate of 50 a year. The movement was further assisted by the General Turnpike Act of 1773 which drew attention to the impossibility of maintaining through routes while local variations still existed, and just as important, which extended provision for money to be raised by taxation for the repair of roads.

The toll system, always unpopular and a constant challenge to travellers determined to avoid paying the dues, was nevertheless a very worthwhile evil.

In 1698 Celia Fiennes noted: 'Thence I went to Windham ....

The Attleborough Dial turnpike stone, drawn before restoration.

mostly on a causey, the county being low and morrish and the road on the causey was in many places full of holes, tho' it is secured by a barr at which passengers may pay a penny a horse in order to the mending of the roads, for all about is not to be rode on unless in a dry summer . . . .'

However, after an early start in Norfolk progress became slow. There was a gap of over a hundred years, for example, between the construction of a stretch of turnpike near Wymondham and the opening of the Fakenham turnpike. Again, some of the main roads never were turnpiked, and some were turnpiked only in part. The general quality of the county's main roads, however, was high.

The oldest turnpike in Norfolk, and in some ways one of the oldest in Britain, was the stretch between Wymondham and Attleborough. It was placed on the statute book in 1695 after the draining of Attleborough Mere had resulted in a slightly more direct route between the two. The Attleborough Road, along with the Harwich Road and the Great North Road, was licensed by the first Turnpike Act, but the Great North Road was actually built first.

On its traditional site east of Attleborough on the present A11, The

31

Dial pillar has an inscription dating the bequest of money to the road building to 1675. The actual Act was not passed for another 20 years. The Dial pillar, which used to have a sundial on top, was restored in 1888 and is now (1983) being restored again.

Incidentally, one branch of the East Dereham turnpike which ran to Mattishall had a clause which said that feather-boards had to be erected to prevent horses being frightened by the Honingham waterwheel.

Dates relating to some of the Norfolk turnpikes (generally metalled with rammed gravel or stones) include:

Wymondham to Attleborough, 1695
Hethersett to Wymondham, 1708
Attleborough to Larlingford, 1746/47
Norwich to Hethersett, 1746/47
Norwich to Scole, 1768
Norwich to Yarmouth (via Blofield, Ormesby, Caister), 1769
Norwich to Dereham, 1770
Norwich to Swaffham, 1770
Norwich to Watton, 1770
Norwich to New Buckenham, 1772
Norwich to Holt, 1784
Norwich to Aylsham, 1794
Norwich to North Walsham, 1796
Norwich to Fakenham, 1823
and Wells to Fakenham, 1826

The general unpopularity of the tolls system tends to obscure its achievements. For example, people journeying to Norwich from the Coltishall area were said to have avoided the Crostwick toll by turning off the turnpike at Horstead and going through Frettenham or Spixworth. At the same time, money raised by the tolls helped establish a network of improved roads, and more, slowly turned a multiplicity of muddy tracks into a system of single routes.

It was the development and spread of the railways which wrecked the tolls. Many of the Turnpike Trusts simply went bankrupt. The last one was wound up in 1895. In 1869 a House of Commons committee considered the Norfolk group and decided that New Buckenham, Norwich, Swaffham and Mattishall, Norwich and Watton, and Thetford, should be discontinued; and that the Aylsham and Cromer Trusts should continue for a little longer. One of the last of the local trusts, the Wells and Fakenham, was dissolved in 1881.

Tollhouses, tollgates, toll bridges

Norfolk possessed a number of tollhouses, and a small number remain. The one at Etling Green, east of Dereham, is a well preserved

Reconstruction of a scene at the tollhouse at Etling Green.

example though it looks like an ordinary single storey cottage. Another example (two storeys, with a bay window over the door) is to be found at Little Walsingham, east of the Priory.

If Faden's map of 1797 is to be trusted on the subject then at that time Norfolk possessed about 40 tollgates, though the overall figure is thought to have been much higher.

In 1811 tolls on the Norwich-Aylsham-Cromer turnpike included: coaches (one to six horses) 3d. to 1s. to 1s.3d.; waggon (one to four horses) 3d. to 8d.; cattle 8d. per score; sheep and pigs 4d. per score. By 1834 the St. Benedict's (Norwich) tollgate, which extracted tolls from users of the Norwich to Swaffham road, was charging: 3d. for a coach, landau, barouche, gig and hearse; 4d. for a wain; and 10d a score for cattle.

A toll bridge, unlike a turnpike road, was usually a commercial concern and belonged to a proprietor or company which would make a profit and pay a dividend. A turnpike road, on the other hand, was a public highway managed for the public by trustees or commissioners.

Milestones

The Turnpike Trusts reintroduced milestones, and the first since the days of the Romans was erected on the Dover road in 1663. An Act of

Parliament of 1767 made the trustees of the Thetford and Norwich turnpike responsible for the erection of milestones and signposts, and many of Norfolk's ancient milestones were placed in position in the following hundred years or so. The Dereham turnpike, for example,

East Dereham turnpike milestone.

still retains its stones with metal plaques at several places. Another stone, in the market place, is incribed, 'London 100 miles, Dereham 0', which seems to indicate a bit of town pride, perhaps at the time of the 18th century rebuilding of the market. Milestones on the Norwich to New Buckenham road also carried the distance to London.

On the road north out of Downham Market, at Cannon Square, is a milestone which is inscribed, 'End of the Lynn Southgate Turnpike Trust'. Another interesting example, on the Green at Acle, commemorates the opening of the New Road to Yarmouth in 1831 and is in the form of a monument.

Enclosures

During the 18th and 19th centuries the growth of industry and an

34

Turnpike stone at Downham Market.

The monumental milestone at Acle Green, which commemorates the opening of the New Road to Yarmouth.

improving prospect of work in the cities and towns contributed to the gradual de-population of the countryside. Suddenly there was a need to reorganise agriculture, preferably along 'industrial' lines. In the end waste land and commons were enclosed, marshes drained, scrub cleared and woodland felled.

Enclosure was achieved in three ways: by Act of Parliament, by order of Commissioners with powers to make awards, and by local consent. Private enclosure Acts were costly, so it was the awards system which was to exert the greatest influence on the road network.

The landscape was divided into patterns encased in regularly shaped roads. Whereas the old roads ran around ponds and trees and obstacles, following for the most part the old trails, many of the new roads were like a rigid framework.

An obvious step was to shorten and straighten the byroads, but it was pointed out that many of the byroads had begun life as boundary lines. A way was found around the land charters, however.

Where the rectangular fields of Parliamentary Enclosure replaced open field strips new roads were needed to connect the new holdings with the existing road network. The new roads often followed the geometry of the new boundaries, though they were sometimes poorly connected. One reason was that the enclosure of adjacent parishes might have been a decade apart.

Some new roads did respect ancient boundaries and eccentricities. Again, not every enclosure road was absolutely straight and not every enclosure field was of regular symmetrical proportions; but in general the Commissioners grouped the fields compactly around the new houses. In the space of perhaps two generations the Midlands, for example, was transformed.

At last long distance coaches could pass through populated areas quickly and safely. Towns sprang up beside the new routes. It was all a far cry from the days of gig and light cart, when town roads were repaired with silt from pits dug at convenient distances, when open drains ran through market places, when crossing a road in winter was next to an impossibility and when stepping stones, wooden posts and railings were familiar street furniture.

Examples of enclosure roads in Norfolk are those which run across the old areas of Mousehold Heath north-east of Norwich - otherwise the Salhouse Road and the South Walsham Road. Built about 1820, they replaced winding tracks.

The early part of the 19th century saw road construction accelerate. In 1831, for example, two important new routes opened, Acle New Road to Yarmouth, and the Walpole Cross Keys to Sutton Bridge embankment (which forged a safer and faster link with Lincolnshire, guides having previously been needed to take parties across the fens).

ROADS & TRACKS

Drove roads

As far as Norfolk is concerned, droving, and thus the use of 'drove' roads or 'driftways', seems to have come into being in the post-turnpike period, the main reasons being that the cattle did not like the hard surfaces and the drovers did not like paying the tolls. To the drovers, the turnpikes represented a slow and expensive form of travel. They got round the problem by using unmade lanes and tracks.

Like the pilgrims before them the drovers and their herds also produced a need for facilities such as overnight grazing, lodging and refreshment. At its peak it represented a considerable industry with thousands of head of cattle and sometimes geese being moved across country or from farms and pastures to the markets. In the 1840s Scottish cattle were driven to east Norfolk and re-fattened on the marshes. The herds would then meet up again at the Brick Kiln Inn, Little Plumstead, to prepare for the joint march to London.

The trade began to die in the mid and late 19th century when the railways came, and many of the drovers' inns, some of necessity in remote places, slowly perished.

No specific drove roads are known in Norfolk, though some of today's lanes and tracks were undoubtedly used during the 18th and 19th centuries for droving purposes.

Lanes, trains and cars

It was not until 1888/89 that the new county councils assumed reponsibility for the care of the more important roads. By this time railway company networks were spreading quickly, and only remnants of the tolls system remained.

In the early 1900s - and after experiments with a mixture of tar, gravel and much rolling produced solid and level surfaces free of dust - central government made grants to local authorities for the good of the road system. The enormous increase in travel encouraged by the railways and later supplemented by motor buses, saw further changes between the two world wars with an increase in the number of privately owned vehicles.

The county councils maintained the major roads by a system of roadmen who worked for a number of miles on each side of their house. Other public roads and lanes, however, had to be kept up by the farmers and landowners. Farmers sometimes dug their own pits to obtain gravel for this purpose.

Much of the tarring of those minor roads which were metalled was carried out in the 1930s. Parish councils submitted lists of roads to be tarred, leaving a certain number as green lanes for cattle. It is still possible to see roads with wide spaced hedges and verges with tarmacadam snaking between them, the old cattle width having been

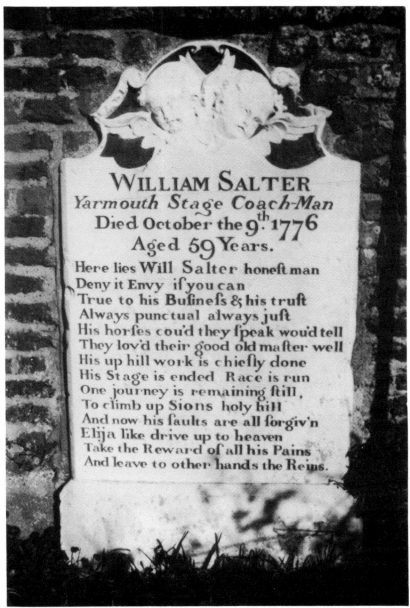

WILLIAM SALTER
Yarmouth Stage Coach-Man
Died October the 9th 1776
Aged 59 Years.

Here lies Will Salter honeſt man
Deny it Envy if you can
True to his Buſineſs & his truſt
Always punctual always juſt
His horſes cou'd they ſpeak wou'd tell
They lov'd their good old maſter well
His up hill work is chiefly done
His Stage is ended Race is run
One journey is remaining ſtill,
To climb up Sions holy hill
And now his faults are all forgiv'n
Elija like drive up to heaven
Take the Reward of all his Pains
And leave to other hands the Reins.

Outside Haddiscoe churchyard.

wider than the area for which money was available for tarring.

Those that were not tarred simply remained as green lanes and are today largely disused except as footpaths or farm access points. They are the 'white roads' on O.S. 1 in. maps. Indeed, of about 10,250 miles (1976) of roads of all kinds in the county, perhaps a third of all these public roads are untarred.

Even so, the origins and dating of many of our (green) lanes remain obscure. A few may be of considerable antiquity, perhaps pre-dating the ownership of the land; and some may have survived because they represent field or parish boundaries. In the main, however, green lanes are simply unmade roads. Prior to the early part of the century, of course, all non-major roads were, in a sense, green lanes. Earlier still, physical boundaries (fences, trees, hedges) became essential to prevent animals straying, and many were built or planted as the surrounding countryside was enclosed. This is one reason why lane boundaries were deemed the responsibility of the landowner.

In 1920 a Ministry of Transport appeared on the scene and by 1936 trunk roads had become its responsibility. The 1930s also saw the building of the Kingston bypass, Britain's first major new road of modern times; and the Norwich ring road, which was one of the first in the country.

For only the third time in history the road system was beginning to be modified and improved by national planning rather than by haphazard local development.

The popular availability of the car after the 1939/45 war produced yet another explosion of ownership which in the 1950s began to place the road network once again under considerable strain.

It has been pointed out before that improvements to roads more often than not lead to the generation of additional traffic which in turn leads to demands for even more improvements. The syndrome certainly had an effect in the 1960s, a decade which saw the start of motorway construction.

Since then the building of bypasses has also proceeded apace, this last development representing an attempt to carry through-traffic away from centres of population. It is interesting to recall that only a few years ago Wendling, Fransham and Necton were on the main A47 (Norwich to King's Lynn) route. The advent of bypasses for Swaffham and Dereham, however, has taken the main route away from those places. Some redundant sections of the former A47 route are already 'preserved' as laybys and gravel dumps.

It remains to be seen if the third great age of road building is coming to an end; but there are signs, mainly financial, that this may be so.

Sacred
To the Memory of
JOHN FOX
who on the 20. of Dec? 1806
in the 79th Year of his Age was
unfortunately kill'd near this spot
having been thrust down & trampled
on by the Horses of a Waggon Tho
his Life was humble yet is it deserving
of imitation He was a worthy & useful
Member of Society an honest
& industrious Labourer
READER
If thou drivest a team be careful
& endanger not the Life of
another or thine own

At Colney church (left).
At Rackheath church (below).

✝
TO THE GLORY OF GOD AND IN SACRED MEMORY OF
MURIEL F. J. BIDWELL.
CHORISTER OF THIS CHURCH WHO WAS MORTALLY INJURED BY A MOTOR CAR & ENTERED PARADISE 10TH DEC 1925 AGED 11 YEARS.
THIS TABLET WAS ERECTED BY PARISHIONERS AND FRIENDS

Metal Detectors

Found objects, other than those of gold and silver, belong to the owner of the land and not to the tenant or finder. Gold and silver objects are subject to a Treasure Trove inquest and must be reported to the local Coroner, though this can be done for you by the local museum. It is important to remember that all land belongs to someone, and prior permission to use a metal detector is thus required. Metal detector users are encouraged to report their finds to the Norfolk Museums Service so that objects of interest can be recorded. Sensible use of metal detectors is to be welcomed, and a pamphlet ('Archaeological finds: some suggestions about the use of metal detectors in Norfolk and Suffolk') has been compiled by the Scole Archaeological Committee. Copies are available from the Norfolk Archaeological Unit, Union House, Gressenhall, East Dereham. In addition, a number of special clubs for detector users have been formed. Ask the Unit for details.

Organisations to join

Norfolk and Norwich Archaeological Society, Garsett House, St. Andrews Hall Plain, Norwich, NR3 1AT

Great Yarmouth & District Archaeological Society, c/o Central Library, Great Yarmouth

West Norfolk & King's Lynn Archaeological Society, c/o Kings's Lynn Museum, King's Lynn

Norfolk Industrial Archaeology Society, c/o The Bridewell Museum, Norwich

Norfolk Archaeological Rescue Group, c/o Norfolk Archaeological Unit, Union House, Gressenhall, East Dereham, NR20 4DR

The Peddars Way Association, c/o 6 Atthill Road, Norwich

(A list of other local societies is usually available from the information service, Norwich Central Library, Bethel Street, Norwich).

Index

ROADS & TRACKS